Basics of Project Management
By Eric Kasten, PMP

Copyright © 2012 by Eric A. Kasten

ALL RIGHTS RESERVED

Cover design by Therese Joanis

To my family and friends, thank you for making life so wonderful.

To the reader, thank you for purchasing my book and supporting me as a writer.

Visit my website: www.kasteneric.com

Basics of Project Management Chapters
1. Introduction
2. Software
3. Planning
4. Task/Checklists
5. Change
6. Scheduling
7. Communication
8. Meetings
9. Risk
10. Faults in your project
11. Conflicts and Resistance
12. Lessons Learned
13. Putting it all Together
14. Project Metrics

1. Introduction

There's no secret for success as a project manager (PM); it takes effort. With the right skills and persistence, project managers will be successful. Let me reiterate... a LOT of persistence. I define 'successful' as influencing the best possible outcome for a project. In a majority of cases, that means achieving 100% of the project's goals. But there are instances where outside factors can hinder achievement of those goals. This book intends to identify the skills and traits necessary for success and how to apply them. The aim of the text is to encourage initiative by the PM, find the best method to motivate others and discuss the tools necessary to complete a project.

This book is intended for beginners in the project management field, but can also benefit experienced project managers.. The focus is on individuals in an organization where established project management practices are not necessarily in place already. This author's first project management experience was in such an environment and my progression from that first project into my full time employment as a project manager is the underlying basis for this book. On the other hand, if you are new to project management but are in an environment where there are established project management practices, this book will serve to support your efforts in that environment. In either case, you will benefit from the skills outlined and the experiences shared. It is this author's experience that even in an environment where project management principles are already applied that the principles are sometimes ignored, and project managers sometimes loose sight of the initiative required to be successful.

In the world of project management, PMI (Project Management Institute) is an accepted authority and an acknowledged certifier of project managers. Project managers certified by PMI gain PMP (Project Management

Professional) certification. This certification must be renewed every three years through continuing education and continuous project management practice. If you are pursuing a career in project management I highly recommend learning more about PMI. Their website is www.pmi.org and this author is a PMP. This book is designed to provide simplified, entry-level instruction into the magical, mystical world of project management. This book is not a re-wording of everything PMI offers, but it does reference PMI occasionally.

Since the first edition of this book was published, I have managed more projects and a wider variety of projects. This experience is being used to expand the content of this book and provide a wider area of knowledge for the reader.

What is a project manager (PM)?

A project manager administers (manages) projects. A PM, in most cases, should not be 'doing' the work, but in some cases 'doing' the work may be required to get the job done. PMs use influencing skills, communication skills, organizational skills and leadership skills in addition to the PM knowledge itself. A successful PM takes ownership and has a vision for the project. PMs must use that vision to motivate the doers to meet the project milestones. PMI's definition of project management is "the application of knowledge, skills and techniques to execute projects effectively and efficiently. Project management is a strategic competency for organizations, enabling them to tie project results to business goals — and thus to better compete in their markets." There are too many types of projects to capture them all effectively, but they all have the same progression of steps to take. As listed on PMI's website, the processes are initiation, planning, execution, monitoring, and control and closing.

Initiation can be as simple as a manager telling you to PM a project, or it can be as complex as finding project sponsors and gaining funding. For the purpose of this book I will simplify the 'initiation' step.

Planning, execution, monitoring and control and closing will be addressed directly and indirectly throughout the chapters.

Chapter 1 takeaway
- This book is focused on beginners in project management
- The assumption is that the project manager's organization has some project management structure established.
- This book also serves as a great refresher for the experienced project manager.

- Project Management Institute (www.pmi.org) is an excellent source of information for developing and enriching your project management skills.
- Plan, execute, monitor and control, and close.

2. Software

All projects consist of many steps, require multiple resources and need coordination with numerous departments. Because of this complexity, you will likely be using some sort of software to manage and track your project. The purpose for software is to provide a level of automation for managing all the dates, tasks, notes, etc... generated by your project and in some cases to generate reports as well. Keeping historical dates and tracking progress with well-written notes is very important when it becomes necessary to escalate issues to a higher level of management, or justify a missed date.

The automation provided by project management software is very valuable. When a date on a current task is changed, the software updates all the dates in the downstream tasks instantly. This shows the downstream effect of delaying a task or completing a task early. It shows where the critical path of a project lies and the overall impact to the project. This "instant effect" allows the PM to analyze potential dates, reply to changes in scope and to report to stakeholders.

There are several major software tools a PM may encounter. It's important to be aware of these since you may encounter them, or ones similar to them. But there's one main tool that stands out (Microsoft Excel) because it is readily available and it is very flexible in terms of its use. Most importantly, any of these software tools can be successfully used by the PM, either alone or together.

Many large companies have large PM organizations (PMOs), and they seek to streamline reporting and increase consistency between the PMs. There's quite a variety of inter-dependencies associated with reporting and measurements of projects, all of which are outside the scope of this book. But the fundamental idea is that organizations want PMs from different areas (geographical areas, departmental areas, etc...)

to use the same, proven steps to achieve success. So, Joe Smith in California and Becky Sue in North Carolina both need to use the same PM plan (steps, checklists, etc…) and the same PM software. This increases the chance of success and equalizes best practices across the organization. The use of the same software generates consistent reports so that upper management can comprehend the status of the projects across the organization and, ultimately, provide insight into how well projects have aligned with the corporate goals.

Alignment with corporate goals is most important. Alignment dictates where funds are allocated for maximum positive effect. It also aligns smaller market level projects with the larger national level projects a corporation may be working on. Or, to put it into a different perspective, it aligns smaller projects that support the completion of larger projects. An example might be completing roadway projects, waterway projects and electrical projects prior to building a neighborhood or shopping center. Each of the projects would be managed by a PM and a Program Manager would oversee the alignment of all projects towards the completion of the whole.

Real life example: After beginning a new PM role where each PM managed several hundred projects, an Excel tool was created to help organize the many sites according to their stage in the project, according to any missed date and according to any defect that affects each project. This Excel tool was slowly picked up and used by other project managers because there was no existing tool that helped manage the projects the way this tool did. The corporate IT team soon incorporated the concepts of the Excel tool into the existing web based tool.

Microsoft Project (MS Project)

Microsoft Project (MS Project) is a common software tool and is widely available for Microsoft operating systems. It does a great job of showing the progress of a project, tracking all the tasks and dates associated with completing a project and providing reports. This tool shows the critical path, has numerous charts for viewing data and provides immediate downstream changes when a current date is changed. This author has used MS Project and would use it again. The problem with this tool, in the large organizations, is that most others do not use it which makes sharing difficult. Also, organizations themselves may have their own required tools for managing projects. When an organization has other tools for managing projects, MS Project just becomes another place to enter the same data already entered somewhere else. This product is very useful, but it is most useful in specific situations where corporate PM tools do not already exist.

Corporate Tools

Very large organizations sometimes have multiple software tools specific to each major portion of a project. There could be a tool specific to funding, purchase orders and quotes. Another tool could be specific to planning and forecasting. There could be several tools to generate different types of tickets for executing work, tracking and measuring timeframes, etc... In a perfect world these multiple tools would all communicate with each other, share data and improve the PM's efficiency. Sometimes they do, and sometimes they do not.

Some of the corporate PM tools are similar to MS Project, others consist of a checklist only, and others may be even simpler. The different flavors of PM tools are vast. As a PM, you will have to make the most out of each tool you are provided with.

Smaller organizations may or may not use the same process or software tools as those used by large organizations. An efficient, smaller organization may have a history of focusing on project management and may use the same software tools that a large organization would. But, small organizations that are not project management focused, or do not have a history of project management will likely allow the PM to choose whatever software they want to use.

Even with mandatory, and good, corporate tools, Many PMs still use MS Excel to some extent. Excel was used to filter dates or categories, used to create a specific report or chart, or to create automation with macros.

Real life example: A large corporation had an online tool for managing project dates and status. Each project consisted of a list of locations that dynamically changed week to week. Each change required resending the list of locations to several organizations and all had different requirements on how the location information be formatted. Excel was used to automatically compile and format the location information for each organizational recipient. Ultimately the Excel tool used to do this was shared nationally.

MS Excel

The most common software used by PMs is Microsoft Excel (MS Excel). Even in a large corporation with many corporate tools being used, MS Excel is still the "go to" tool. It's used for tracking checklists, dates, tasks, lists… you name it. No matter how many corporate tools a large organization has, they still use a large amount of MS Excel spreadsheets. There's simply no escaping it.

If you're not a strong MS Excel user, brush up on your skills. You will be using MS Excel a lot as a PM. Acquiring efficiency in functions, formatting, pivot tables, etc… in this program will make your life much easier. Once you master a few Excel tricks, the others will come to you easily. Soon you will be using Excel with skillful efficiency.

This author has experience with projects requiring two separate PM tools be maintained simultaneously and MS Excel was still a necessity to keep dates straight, document notes, etc… The point is, get experienced with MS Excel!

Another form of project management with MS Excel is database dumps to Excel. These are generally large spreadsheets with project information on the left and columns of dates to the right. This use of Excel usually results in daily spreadsheets being distributed with the newest dates. In this example, the PM is managing through dates. Look for dates that are past due and look for dates that can be pulled in.

Macros! Learn macros. To eliminate manual and repetitive tasks, macros are a life saver. Macros are used to manipulate data on the simple end, and to make complicated calculations on the difficult end. Macros can use arrays and other powerful code techniques that amaze most beginner Excel users. Macros can open other files, read data from those files, perform calculations, export the results to another file and send that new file to recipients via email. It is amazingly powerful. The other benefit is that anyone can view a MS Excel file, making distribution very easy and simple.

Custom Tools

The last set of software tools worth mentioning are custom tools. These are the personal tools that some PMs use in addition to MS Excel and the corporate software provided. Microsoft Visual Basic is used to program custom PM tools. This program provides another way to enter data but can still use the required corporate steps to execute projects. And, with custom tools, one can export custom reports to MS Excel for reporting purposes. In a way, it's similar to using MS Excel outside the required corporate software tools, but more automation can be built into Visual Basic. The downside is that newer versions of MS Windows make distribution of executable files difficult, so sharing a Visual Basic tool is not as easy as sharing an Excel file.

Find what is best for your situation

Balance is the key. As a PM you want to optimize your time and simplify your tools. Every PM is different, so every PM will have a different balance point. Your job, as a PM, is to find that sublime balance.

MS Excel, MS Project, corporate software and custom software are all possible tools every PM may use. For new PMs in non project management focused organizations, it is recommend to start with MS Excel. It's easy to set up a simple list of tasks, track dates, create reports and share spreadsheets (because almost everyone has MS Excel nowadays). It's also the one tool you will use in almost any situation. A simple spreadsheet with custom headers such as 'Task', 'Contact', 'Date Started', 'Projected Completion Date', and 'Actual Completion Date' is all you need to start your first project.

Chapter 2 takeaway
- MS Project – A great piece of software focused on managing projects.
- Corporate software – Large organizations may have their own tools for managing projects, reporting, creating tickets, etc…
- MS Excel – Most commonly used tool. Very easy and very powerful.
- Custom software – Sometimes encountered. Mainly used to automate portions of project management. Not as simple as Excel macros.
- Recommended that new PMs start with MS Excel.

A chart showing these PM tools and how they are used in an organization can be found on my website under the Chapter 2 section, at http://www.kasteneric.com/Page6.html.

3. Planning

Joe Smith may have built hundreds of houses and may be able to build them blindfolded, but he still needs a plan. The plan is the roadmap that the project follows to reach the goal. It's also used to set the order for tasks to be completed, identify prerequisites, assign ownership to tasks, and measure progress throughout the project.

Scope

The project scope defines what needs to be accomplished to reach project completion, and defines what the successful completion of the project is. Without a defined scope, the project runs the risk of failure. The more well defined the scope, the greater the chance for success. Scope should also define what completion looks like.

If a future home owner provides a scope of 'build me a home', how does the general contractor know how to define success? Does he build a 1000 square foot home or a 2000 square foot home? Is the home supposed to be 3 bedrooms or 4 bedrooms? How many bathrooms? In terms of project management, the more specific the scope is, the greater the likelihood of success and happiness of the receiver of the project output.

The scope defines when your project is complete. When you match all the parameters stated in your scope statement, you are done. With this you can measure success. The measurement of success is important. It reveals how well you met the requirements. This should be a quantifiable measurement too, whenever possible.

You, as the PM, must determine how specific your scope definition needs to be. Some examples are:

- Move X number of equipment type Y, from equipment rack A to equipment rack B before Date D.
- Build a 2400 sq. ft. house with 4 bedrooms and 3 bathrooms. Bedroom 1 shall be X sq. ft. Bedrooms 2, 3 and 4 shall be Y sq. ft. Kitchen shall include granite countertops a brass faucet model number 12345 and be Z sq. ft. large. etc…
- Add a 400 sq. ft. deck to the back of my house. It shall be 20 ft. by 20 ft. and include stairs on the east side, leading to the ground below. Railings should be 42", per code. Electric should be run to 3 outlets, one centered on each side and deck should be made of pressure treated wood 24" above ground.

Scope Creep

What if the future home owner changes his request from a 3 bedroom to a 4 bedroom and adds a garage? That's called scope creep and causes the general contractor (PM) to re-evaluate the project and to introduce 'change requests' (discussed in Chapter 5).

Scope creep is when the scope is slowly increased, or changed, to encompass more than what was originally agreed upon. Sometimes a change in scope may not affect the project dates, but a significant change in scope will affect project dates. Your responsibility is to measure the scope change's effect on the project and, if the project's completion timeline is negatively impacted, to re-negotiate the project. In some cases the project completion date will be extended and/or the project may need additional funding to be completed. Normally an increase in scope will result in an increase in time and/or cost.

When the project scope changes, a new baseline of tasks will need to be developed. This results in changes to scheduled dates to match the new scope. This must be done in order to accurately reflect completion of all tasks and to accurately set expectations for everyone who has a stake in the project. Do not project manage your self into failure.

"Baseline" is mentioned above. A baseline is a set of initial target dates assigned to tasks. The baseline dates are the initial expected completion dates of tasks. These baselines are used to measure variations in new dates if a date is forced to change. It is also used to measure the actual completion date of a task. If a task baseline completion date is 8/1/2018 and the forecasted completion date is forced to change to 8/10/2018 due to a delivery delay, this 9 day variation is easily identified. That variation can then be used to check if it will have an overall negative impact on the project, or to track total delays. The baseline can also be used to measure how far off the expected completion is from the actual completion of a task. If a task is expected to complete 3/1/2019 and it is actually completed on 3/6/2019, there is a 5 day variation that needs to be looked into to discover the root cause of the delay and the overall impact to the project.

Tasks/Timelines/Resources

Part of the planning process is to identify all the tasks, timelines and resources involved in completing a project. Unless one has expertise in the required tasks of the project, this is best completed by involving subject matter experts and others who are actually involved in the project. This can be done by either setting up a conference call or by a face-to-face meeting. It helps to start this meeting with an outline of the project scope and any guidelines the project must follow. From there, allow an open, but guided, discussion of how to achieve the project goals. During the meeting, you should record the tasks (steps), resources and timelines required to complete the project and, at the end of the meeting, go through the tasks again to confirm that everyone agrees on what the group created and who owns each task.

A sample list of tasks, task owners and timelines for building a house (version 1):
1. Building permit – General Contractor – 14 days
2. Foundation – Joe's Cement Co. – 7 days
3. Framing and walls – Jimmy's Framers – 21 days
4. Roof – Top Roofing Co. – 7 days
5. Plumbing – Al's Plumbing Co. – 14 days
6. Electrical – Bert's Electrical Co. – 14 days
7. Doors and Windows – Prairie Window and Door Co. – 7 days
8. Inspections – County Inspector – 5 days
9. Interior walls – Wally's Drywall Co. – 14 days
10. Kitchen/bathrooms – Smith's Cabinets – 14 days
11. Fit and finish – General Contractor – 7 days
Total days = 124 days

The above lists each task, the resource which will own the work and the days required to complete each step (a simple timeline).

If all tasks were performed in sequence (one after another, without overlap), the project would take 124 days. At this point the PM should begin looking for opportunities to complete tasks in parallel (completing more than one task at the same time). For example, the electrical and plumbing could take place at the same time, but not before the roof is complete. Therefore, the plumbing and electrical are said to be dependent upon the completion of the roof.

If the project started January 1st, and we add in the start and end dates of the tasks, we have the following.

A sample list of tasks for building a house (version 2):

1. Jan 1 – Jan 14 : Building permit – General Contractor – 14 days
2. Jan 15 – Jan 21 : Foundation – Joe's Cement Co. – 7 days
3. Jan 22 – Feb 11 : Framing and walls – Jimmy's Framers – 21 days
4. Feb 12 – Feb 18 : Roof – Top Roofing Co. – 7 days
5. Feb 19 – March 4 : Plumbing – Al's Plumbing Co. – 14 days
6. Feb 19 – March 4 : Electrical – Bert's Electrical Co. – 14 days
7. March 5 – March 11 : Doors and Windows – Prairie Window and Door Co. – 7 days
8. March 12 – March 15 : Inspections – County Inspector – 5 days
9. March 16 – March 29 : Interior walls – Wally's Drywall Co. – 14 days
10. March 30 – April 12 : Kitchen/bathrooms – Smith's Cabinets – 14 days
11. April 13 – April 19 : Fit and finish – General Contractor – 7 days

Total days = 110 days

With tasks 5 and 6 being worked in parallel, our total days drop from 124 days (version 1) to 110 days. These are the types of task and resource optimization you are expected to perform as a project manager.

When the timeline is set by a project sponsor or other factor, you may have to work backwards from the predefined deadline and find additional opportunities to reduce the total days for project completion.

Project Sponsor

The project sponsor could be a boss, another department, upper management, or yourself. The sponsor is typically the person who initiates, provides funding for and champions the project. The sponsor sees the need for the project to be completed and provides support to complete the project. There's always someone or something driving a project.

Task Ownership

It is important to identify resources in order to identify ownership of tasks. Without task ownership the PM can end up with two or more people (groups) pointing fingers at each other, instead of getting the work completed. Clarity of task ownership and clarity of task schedule are both critical components of planning.

Real life example: One project clearly identified the group responsible for completing a task. However the group identified was not contacted by the program manager who assigned them to the task. When they were contacted to complete their assigned task, they scoffed and resisted prioritizing the project work over their own work. The situation had to be escalated and their work negotiated in order for the project to move forward.

Chapter 3 takeaway
- Define project scope. This tells you when the project is finished and if it was successful or not.
- Document changes to the scope and re-baseline. Renegotiate time and/or cost.
- Identify and work with project sponsor.
- Record tasks, resources and timeline (start/end dates).
- Create ownership.

A sample task list, in MS Excel format, can be found on my website under the Chapter 3 section, at http://www.kasteneric.com/Page6.html.

4. Task/Checklists

A major part of planning to ensure project success is in identifying the tasks, or steps, to complete a project and in creating checklists. As described in the previous chapter, tasks identify the steps needed to complete a project and the schedule provides the order in which they need to be completed. Checklists help detail those tasks.

Subject Matter Experts

When initiating a new project, you need to identify and engage the subject matter experts (SMEs). The SMEs must be engaged to provide the knowledge and details that you do not have. This is also a great opportunity for you to gain knowledge and perspective on the project. It also motivates the SMEs, giving them some "skin in the game" and a sense of ownership in the project. Document their names, areas of expertise and their contact information as part of the project resources.

The other benefit of engaging the SMEs at an early stage is that it gives you, the PM, a chance to evaluate your scope. If the SMEs identify more work than can be accomplished before the project is to be completed, it's early enough in the project to renegotiate the due date for completing the project or, at a minimum, identify the inability to achieve the existing due date. If renegotiating dates is not possible, the PM should document the issue as a 'jeopardy to the project' (more on this in chapter 11).

Once you have your SMEs in a meeting together, providing input and brainstorming, record everything. Write it on an overhead projector, on a whiteboard, on your laptop connected to a projector... Let the SMEs see the notes as you write them. Oftentimes the discussion of one task may trigger an 'Oh yeah' moment and they will return to an earlier task to provide additional detail that is critical to the project. Be transparent with your notes, your tasks and how you plan to organize the tasks. Don't forget to ask questions; questions are a great way to gain additional understanding as well as to discover hidden tasks that the SMEs might take for granted. Project management is not about putting blinders on and going it alone; it's about involving the right people and working as a team to accomplish a goal. The PM acts as the leader of that team.

The SMEs need to provide an order to the tasks; chronological order is usually best. Part of the reason for establishing the order of tasks is to determine which must be completed in series and which tasks can be completed in parallel. Parallel is always preferred because it allows more than one task to be completed at a time, ultimately speeding up the project.

Real life example: In a project years ago, the project stakeholder instructed the PM to not engage the SME for a specific piece of hardware. When the SME found out there was a project to deploy more of his equipment, but he was not involved, the SME was furious. The SME was ultimately pulled into the project meetings, but never fully supported the project and kept tossing unnecessary wrenches into the project.

Predecessor and Milestone

Two other terms important to PMs are predecessor and milestone.
1. Predecessor defines which task must be completed prior to the start of the next task. For example, the frame of a house has to be completed before the electrical wires can be run… so framing is a predecessor to electrical.
2. A milestone is a major accomplishment within the project… bigger than a task, but smaller than

completion of the project. Typically, common tasks can be grouped together to create a milestone. For example, if a project involves connecting two pieces of computer equipment, the completed preparation of equipment A would be a milestone. The completed preparation of equipment B would be a second milestone. When the two pieces of equipment are finally connected, the project would be complete. A project would be organized so that when all milestones are completed, the project is complete.

Now our sample project for building a house looks like (version 3):
1. Milestone: Basic structure complete (Jan 1 – Feb 18)
    a. Jan 1 – Jan 14 : Building permit – General Contractor – 14 days
    b. Jan 15 – Jan 21 : Foundation – Joe's Cement Co. – 7 days
    c. Jan 22 – Feb 11 : Framing and walls – Jimmy's Framers – 21 days
    d. Feb 12 – Feb 18 : Roof – Top Roofing Co. – 7 days
2. Milestone: Prepare to close walls (Feb 19 – March 15)
    a. Feb 19 – March 4 : Plumbing – Al's Plumbing Co. – 14 days
    b. Feb 19 – March 4 : Electrical – Bert's Electrical Co. – 14 days
    c. March 5 – March 11 : Doors and Windows – Prairie Window and Door Co. – 7 days
    d. March 12 – March 15 : Inspections – County Inspector – 5 days
3. Milestone: Close walls and complete construction (March 16 – April 19)
    a. March 16 – March 29 : Interior walls – Wally's Drywall Co. – 14 days
    b. March 30 – April 12 : Kitchen/bathrooms – Smith's Cabinets – 14 days

  c. April 13 – April 19 : Fit and finish – General Contractor – 7 days

Total days = 110 days

Milestone 1 is a prerequisite to Milestone2. Milestone 2 is a prerequisite to Milestone3. Milestones help organize the tasks and allow for a sense of achievement as the project progresses.

Checklists

Along with tasks, checklists are great tools for the PM. Checklists identify the specific, often minute, details that need to be "checked off" before a larger task can be completed, or before another task can be started. For example, Milestone 3, task b is kitchens/bathrooms… A checklist that could be used to determine if this task was ready to be started would look similar to this.

3. b. Kitchen/Bathrooms Checklist
  1. Before task can start
    a. Drywall complete in kitchen
    b. Drywall complete in bathrooms
    c. Sink drains exposed, ready
    d. Sink hot/cold water exposed/ready
    e. Toilet drain in correct location
  2. To identify as complete
    a. Tiling complete, inspected, and accepted
    b. Cabinets installed per layout
    c. Cabinet doors installed
    d. Sinks installed
    e. Hot/Cold water correct
    f. Sinks drain
    g. Appliances installed in kitchen

This checklist lets one know exactly when task 3. b. can be started and when it can be marked off as completed.

Depending on the complexity of your project, the tasks and checklists can be simple, or very complex.

Real life example: Several projects have consisted of checklists as the sole documentation, at the direction of the Program Management team. These checklists were very easy to use and status was easily determined. The checklists were archived, but nothing else was documented and all communication was via email or phone call.

Broad view to Narrow view

Not all projects start with every detail ironed out right from the start. At the beginning it is acceptable to have less detail on later tasks. As tasks get closer to starting, the details need to be narrowed down. As the project progresses, more information is gained and later tasks should then be detailed. For example, when starting to build a new house and the foundation is being poured, the PM doesn't need to know what light fixtures will be installed next to the front door. But once the siding is going up, the PM should already know exactly which light fixtures are being installed on the exterior of the house.

Tickets

Some organizations use tickets (or ticketing systems) to assign which individual or group performs specific tasks. For example, a ticket may need to be issued in a technical company to have a cable connected between two ports. When tickets are involved, the PM must record who is responsible for creating the ticket, when the ticket must be created in order to allow enough time to complete the task, ticket due date and the ticket number. These four items need to be recorded in the project plan, either within the associated task, or on a separate ticket tracker, or both.

More on MS Project and MS Excel

MS Project will automatically update the project for you when you enter prerequisite information. The program also makes it easy to create milestones. MS Excel requires you to do these activities manually since it does not have project management functionality built into it. But, MS Excel is still a very good tool for managing a project and for using checklists. It's easy to use a separate tab for tasks, checklists, resource/contact lists, etc…

Chapter 4 takeaway
- Engage SMEs early in the project to establish the tasks, predecessors, milestones and checklists.
- SMEs are important resources to your project. Document who they are and their contact information.
- Document a risk that negatively affects project success as a 'jeopardy' to the project.
- Predecessor defines which task needs to be completed before another task can be started.
- A milestone is a major accomplishment within the project, comprised of similar tasks.
- Broad tasks in beginning… narrow in on specifics as project progresses.
- Record all ticket numbers, responsible ticket creator, ticket creation date and ticket due date.
- Project management is not about putting blinders on and going it alone; it's about involving the right people and working as a team to accomplish a goal. The PM acts as the leader of that team.

Sample task list (version 2) in MS Excel format, which is the schedule with milestones added, can be found on my website. The checklist for task 3.b. can also be found on my website.

27

Both are under the Chapter 4 section, at
http://www.kasteneric.com/Page6.html.

5. Change

As the old saying goes, "the only constant is change". An important aspect of project management is tracking change. When you're lucky, the project moves forward without much deviation from the plan, but often times, internal or external factors force change into your project.

As stated before, setting the scope is important in order to know when the project is complete and to know if you were successful or not. Having a defined scope is also important for tracking the changes against that scope and the ultimate impact of each change on your project.

Change Request

As simple as it sounds, this is a request for a change to the project. It should be treated as only a request, not as a given. A change request is a form filled out by someone who is requesting that change. A large project should include a formal change request form and process. On smaller projects, it's also possible for your change request process to be as simple as sending an email and holding a meeting about the requested change. The change requests should be tracked in a log. They can be reviewed either individually as they occur or on a regular time basis

When a change is proposed, the requestor is submitting a change request. This is simply a request for a change to the scope of the project. It should be up to you, the PM, and the project sponsor to consider if the change request is accepted or not. If accepted, the change request could cause either a significant alteration of the project scope, or a minor one. In all cases, the scope needs to be adjusted, the proper funding allocated and the project tasks/schedule updated to reflect the incorporation of the change.

It is also possible for the change to result in a reduction of project scope.

Positive or Negative Change

The first thing to do when a change is introduced is to determine if it is a positive or negative change. Positive change may be a reduction in quantity of equipment, or a reduction to the size of a house. The positive change may then allow you to reduce your project time and or cost, sometimes not. A negative change is just the opposite. It is something that will extend the timeframe and/or cost of a project, such as an increase in square footage of a house. A positive change should be treated the same as a negative change and both should be reviewed. Not all positive changes are accepted.

There is always the possibility that a change can not be incorporated into a project. Financial, quality, cost and function are all common factors taken into account when considering a change request. Any of these, or any other, may be enough to reject the request.

If a project is far enough along that a change would be too significant to incorporate, the change request may have to be noted and rejected. In this case the change request should be discussed at the end of the project. Either the change request will be discarded, set up as a new project, or incorporated into another project. The PM, project sponsor and stakeholders would have to make a decision about how to treat this type of change.

Review, Document and Communicate

When a change is accepted and incorporated into a project, the tasks, checklists, schedule and resources may change. A review of the project is needed by the SMEs and any change needs to be clearly identified and communicated to everyone.

When communication is sent out, the PM is responsible for clearly communicating what the change is and its impact on the project.

There are several ways to document a change. A change log can be kept on a separate MS Excel tab. This is effective for tracking the date, description and effect of each change. The simplest way to document changes is to keep an email trail. Although this is not the most efficient or productive way to track changes, it is sometimes effective for small projects, small changes, or when there are only a few changes. As the PM, you will need to determine the method that works best for you and your project.

Real life example: At the end of one project, the results were less than expected. The changes were well documented throughout the project and The PM was able to add the significant changes to the final project summary. The PM was ultimately congratulated on how well they adapted to the changes and how they were still be able to complete the project.

Chapter 5 takeaway
- Determine whether a change is positive or negative. Then determine whether the change will affect your project in a significant way.
- If project scope is affected, communicate and request appropriate changes.
- Communicate the change and its impact on the project.
- Consider change requests and their impact on the project.
- Document. Document. Document.

6. Scheduling

If you've read the first five chapters, you've already been introduced to the basics of scheduling. Determining how long a task will take to complete and adding dates to your project is all part of scheduling. A PM would have some measure of success if task duration and task dates were all that were spelled out.

Process time and Cycle time

In a perfect world, the drywall company would show up exactly when needed and finish exactly when they said they would finish. Since this isn't a perfect world, you have to consider process time versus cycle time. These are actually lean six sigma processes, but they apply quite effectively to simple project management. Lean six sigma is the method of continually improving processes.

1. Cycle time is defined as the amount of time required to complete a task from the time the task is assigned to an individual, to the time the task is completed. If you drop your car off at a gas station to have a tire changed, cycle time is the amount of time it takes for the gas station to change your tire and return it to you. When the car is dropped off at 1pm and the car is returned to you at 3pm, the cycle time is 2 hours. Cycle time is calculated by subtracting the time the task is assigned from the time the task is completed and the next task can start. Since you do not have your car returned to you until 3pm, the task completion is marked as 3pm.
2. Process time is the amount of time it takes to complete a task when the person doing the task is focused solely on that task. If it takes a person 30 minutes to change a tire, when the only task that person is doing is changing that tire, the process time is 30 minutes. So even though it takes 2 hours for you to get your car back from the gas station, it only took 30 minutes to complete the task. This is the difference between process time and cycle time.

In the new house examples used in previous chapters, cycle time was used when assigning timeframes. Timeframes can most accurately be determined and assigned by going to the source of each task.. In the house example the source would be the people/companies doing the work. Sometimes an experienced PM can make an educated guess on both cycle time and process time. Other times, the people completing the task may have a standard Service Level Agreement (SLA). In the case of an SLA, you will have to use that SLA timeframe.

It's important to know the cycle time as well as the process time. If you have 2 weeks cycle time assigned to complete drywall (3. a. March 16 – March 29 : Interior walls – Wally's Drywall Co. – 14 days), but the process time is only 1 week, you may be able to overlap this task with the task before it, or the task after it… reducing your timeline.

The other benefit of knowing and measuring the process times and cycle times is to identify areas of improvement or optimization, as well as identifying abnormalities.

If a cycle time is two weeks and the process time is two hours, there could be adjustments made to reduce the cycle time. And any good PM worth their salt would work to reduce that cycle time.

Tracking process and cycle times is not necessary for beginner PMs, or small projects. These are important concepts to keep in mind during execution of your project. If you want to, or need to, move into more complex projects and increase your PM skills, these two concepts are useful. And, if you happen to perform similar projects, these two concepts can be carried over from one project to another. Using this knowledge could make you a super hero.

Service Level Agreement

The SLA is often used in large organizations where the team or individual responsible for the work has numerous groups requesting task completion. The SLA provides adequate time for the team or person to complete the tasks in order of priority or in the order they were submitted. It also provides a standard cycle time so that projects can be scheduled faster and with less effort. The downsize is that the schedule has excess time built into it. For example, a national team may be the only ones who work on a specific type of equipment and that equipment resides in every city in the country. The national team could receive requests from many cities to make changes to the equipment. The SLA would provide the national team enough time to complete the multiple requests and it would provide a timeline for completion so that planners in each city know how long the work takes without the national team having to provide a status to all projects.

In the case of SLAs, you may not be able to measure process time separately from cycle time and you may have no flexibility to perform tasks in parallel. As the PM, you will have to approach each task individually and decide the best approach.

Real life example: During a project that needed an SLA shortened, the PM made a phone call to the engineer assigned to the work. The engineer completed the work while on the phone with the PM. This saved the PM 3 days.

Conflicting Activities

Lets say you have a router sitting in Chicago and your project involves performing a software upgrade on this router. Do you just set a date and do your upgrade blindly? Or do you coordinate with other departments and the team responsible for 'owning' the router? It is entirely possible that another department within your company is planning to do a hardware upgrade at the same time as your software upgrade, or another department could be planning to connect another piece of equipment to the same router at the same time as your software upgrade. These factors are outside your control and the priority of which takes place first, would have to be worked out with all involved.

This is where communication is critical and this is where changes to the project schedule are introduced. As the PM, you must reach out (communicate) with other teams to make sure your project schedule and their schedules do not conflict. Hopefully there is only one person, or team, responsible for coordinating activities affecting the router, but that's not always the case.

There are work management tools (Scheduling tools) that require entering a ticket into a system in order to perform some work function on equipment. This tool identifies conflicts and provides contacts for those conflicts. This tool can become very complex by also identifying downstream equipment that may be affected when work is performed on the original equipment.

If a conflict is discovered, there are several ways to work around the conflict. You could use first-in-first out (FIFO), schedule by priority, or schedule based on whose project has the most flexibility, etc… If your project happens to be the one that is delayed, you now have to re-baseline and communicate.

Resources

In addition to making sure that there are no conflicting activities on the router, you need to also make sure you have someone available to do the work for you. Just because the equipment is not being worked on by anyone else, doesn't mean that there are resources (SME, technician, engineer, etc…) available to do the work.

You may need a ticket to reserve the needed resource that will perform your software upgrade, or a confirmation email from that person's manager. Either way, document the ticket and include the manager and resource in your communications and meeting invitations. Keep them informed and keep them involved.

Flexibility

Some projects allow flexibility to be built into the schedule, others may not. Flexibility does not mean 'padding' the schedule so you're always successful. It means building in enough time to successfully complete your project. Sometimes this means accounting for 'unknown risks', sometimes it means starting and finishing early enough to beat your drop dead date (DDD).

DDD is the date that your project must be completed. Your project cannot extend beyond that date without negatively affecting something else (another project, customers, costs, etc…)

There is always the possibility that your project could be behind schedule from the moment it is started and you have no chance of completing the project by the DDD. In this case the project is considered 'dead on arrival' (DOA). The only thing you can do in this case is communicate ("it's physically impossible to complete this project on time") and document (communications, contacts, SME notes, etc…). You can still be a hero if you document and communicate this, yet still not meet the deadline. If you are in this situation and miraculously make the deadline, then will be the super hero.

Chapter 6 takeaway
- Consider cycle time, process times and service level agreements (SLAs) when setting schedule.
- SLA is Service Level Agreement and is a standardized cycle time for PMs to use on their schedule.
- DDD is the date that your project must be completed.
- A DOA project is a 'dead on arrival' project.
- Look for conflicting activities that could interfere with your work.
- Remain flexible.

An example of how equipment and resource activities create scheduling conflicts can be found on my website under the Chapter 6 section, at http://www.kasteneric.com/Page6.html.

7. Communication

Communication not only benefits you, but it also benefits the stakeholders of your project. Your communications inform them of your schedule, of the project's deficiencies and these communications should increase the transparency of your project.

Simplicity

As the PM, you should keep an eye on the needs of your audience. The 'Keep It Simple' method is always the best starting point. As you grow to understand your audience better you can tweak your communication style to better meet their needs. Before sending out an email, ask yourself:

1. Who needs to know this?
    a. Sometimes you need to add a person to an email to resolve an issue, but does that person need to remain on all subsequent emails as well?
    b. Does everyone need to know that you are requesting data from Mr. X?
    c. Does everyone need to know that you are escalating a data request from Mr. X to his boss?
    d. Keep distribution lists to a minimum.
    e. Include anyone requesting to be notified.
2. What information do they need?
    a. A daily project update may not need to have more than current status and an open issues list.
    b. If you're communicating the schedule, do the recipients need to know the resource list and identified risks?
    c. What is important and what is nice to know? Nice to know information may not need to be communicated as frequently, to everyone, or at all.
3. Is this relevant?

  a. Do you need to continue sending out the 'resolved issues list' two months later?
  b. Do you need to identify a task that cannot be started until a month later?
4. Is this too much information?
  a. Can the information be simplified?
  b. Is there redundant information?
  c. Does the information apply solely to your project?
5. How is my grammar?

Receiving too much information in an email reduces the likelihood that anyone will read it. And if the recipients constantly receive too much information, the ones that did read it may stop reading it. Their time is valuable.

Keeping it simple helps you to highlight the most important items and increases visibility where it is needed. Using **bold** text on important items and color coding also helps bring attention where it is needed. Do not over-use these though because then your communication just becomes a cluttered rainbow. Keep it simple.

Charts and graphs are great at painting a picture for the recipient. A chart shows a lot of information in a small area. A graph shows even more than a chart and is much easier to look at (as long as it is simple). If the data that feeds a graph is long and causes the resulting graph to be difficult to decipher, then group data into categories to simplify the graph. For example, if a chart lists the number of days (from 1 to 200) with some result tied to each day count, the resulting bar graph would be very tight from left to right. But if the days were grouped together in weekly chunks (1-7 days, 8-14 days, etc…) the graph would still convey the same message, but would be much easier to view and decipher.

Email chains

The dreaded 'reply to all' email chain is legendary. These email chains clog up the email server and everyone's inbox. As the PM, you need to set the example when you reply to emails. And don't be afraid to instruct email recipients when to reply to all, or when not to reply to all. You can incorporate a brief email policy at the bottom of all your emails too.

"Please reply to all with your response."
"Please do not use reply to all."

When you click reply to all, to respond to an email, consider the recipients. Does each one need to hear your reply or know that you replied? If not, take them off the reply.

Real life example: Someone accidentally used an organizational distribution list in an email that should have been distributed to only a handful of people. Over 50 people replied to all saying, "Please take me off this distribution list."

On the other hand, if someone is left off an email, but you know they should be included, add them to the distribution list. Always make sure the required recipients are included. This saves time and reduces email.

So, Mrs. Y emailed you asking who is responsible for a task on your project... Do you reply to Mrs. Y and say "You need to talk to John G. for that."? Or do you reply to Mrs. Y and copy John G. as well? By copying John G. in your email you cut down on the numbers of overall emails because now Mrs. Y does not have to send yet another email to initiate contact John G. herself. You've just saved Mrs. Y time and you've set the example in hopes that they will do the same for you. You've also just reduced the number of emails flying back-n-forth within your company.

How do you communicate?

When is it best to use email, text, a phone or meet face-to-face? Each has its pros and cons. Sometimes it depends on the importance of the communication and sometimes it depends on the recipient.

Email is a great tool for reaching many people and for documentation. Emails can be read when the recipient has time to read them. This increases the chance that the recipient will read it, but decreases the chances of a quick response. Not everyone takes the time to read all their emails though. Emails need to be structured for easy interpretation and quick identification of important information (remember the 'Keep it simple' idea). The worst part of emails is the lack of 'emotional tone', which may be positive from the sender, but interpreted negatively by the receiver.

Instant messages and text messages (via computer or phone) work well for less important items, but are great for getting a quick response. This type of communication is more personal as well. But, not everyone uses this tool and if someone is away from their desk or phone, the message could sit idle for a long time.

A phone call is always great for immediate response or resolution. Two-way communication is personal and tone is easily interpreted. The phone call can be between two or more people as well. The problem is that a phone call has to be at a specific time and not everyone can accommodate that, or it is instant and not everyone has time at that instant.

Face-to-face is the most personal and builds the best working relationships. This usually takes more time because of pleasantries and the possibility of side conversations. A face-to-face meeting is great for discussions, team meetings, etc…

Chapter 7 takeaway
- Communications… 'Keep It Simple'
- Include everyone that needs to know.
- Control email chains… set the example.
- Add or remove recipients as required.
- Decide the best form of communication.

A chart showing communication pros and cons can be found on my website under the Chapter 7 section, at http://www.kasteneric.com/Page6.html.

8. Meetings

You cannot manage a project without holding meetings. Meetings are critical and allow the team to discuss issues, ask questions, confirm items and coordinate activities. As PM, you will be required to set the agenda and provide control and direction for the meetings.

Kickoff Agenda

When setting the agenda for the project's first meeting, think of it as a kickoff meeting. Most likely you'll want to focus on explaining the purpose for the project, provide a high level schedule, begin identifying resources, and other broad items. There is nothing holding you back from setting detail-oriented agenda items as well. It all depends on your project.

Bullet items or numbers should be used to identify each item on the agenda. This makes it easier to discern each item and to reference each one individually. Make sure that you list the agenda items in the order you will be addressing them and put them in a logical order. It wouldn't be very logical to review the schedule before going over the scope of the project.

A simple Kickoff agenda may look like this:
1. Project purpose and scope
2. Initial schedule
3. Resources required
4. Questions
5. Next meeting notification

Project 'driving' agenda

After the Kickoff meeting is held, you move into the 'driving' section of your project, where you are driving to complete tasks as well as the overall project. These on going meetings will differ from the Kickoff meeting and require a different focus in the agendas.

To complete the project your agendas should contain three sections… and in this order:
1. Follow up from last meeting's agenda items – Inevitably there will be agenda items that are not completed and follow up is necessary. Make sure you always carry over and open items from the past meetings into the current meeting.

    A list of action items should be reviewed at the beginning of each meeting. When a task has not been completed, or a new item is identified for completion, you list these as 'action items'. The action item list identifies actions or tasks that need to be completed, the date it needs to be completed by, and the person responsible for completion of the action item. Ownership is critical, so always make sure you identify the person responsible for completion of the action item. At the same time as assigning ownership, the you must set the date when the action item is due.

2. Review currently due tasks – As time progresses, new tasks will become due. You need to review these new tasks and any associated checklists. If they're complete, mark them as complete; if not, they will be a carry over item for the next meeting.
3. Look forward toward upcoming tasks – Always look at the tasks that will come due in the short-term and long-term view. Some individuals, responsible for completing the upcoming tasks, may not be fully aware of their responsibility or the fact that the date is closing in on them to complete the task. Make sure they have eyes on the task heading their way and that they fully understand their role. Also make sure they

have everything necessary to complete their task (such as a successful hand-off from the predecessor task to the new task).

A sample agenda for a typical driving meeting may look like this:
1. From last meeting
    a. Review action item list from last meeting
    b. Update action item status
    c. Notes/Questions
2. Current tasks
    a. Tasks due now
    b. Task status
    c. Current project status (on track, not on track, etc...)
3. Next week outlook
    a. Tasks coming due next week
    b. Confirm resources are on-track to complete
    c. Questions
4. Review action item list and any incomplete agenda items
5. Open for questions...

End of project agenda

As the project nears completion your focus changes to closing out tasks and checklists... ultimately, closing out the project. The agenda for this type of meeting increases the focus on completion of tasks and action items, as well as stressing any upcoming drop dead dates (DDD) associated with the project. As the project gets closer to the end, there is less room for deviations and more emphasis needs to be placed on completing on time.

This agenda is similar to the 'driving' agenda, but should get more emphasis from the PM and, in the event there's a lingering issue, any escalations should be reviewed at the beginning of the meeting. Escalations are covered more thoroughly in Chapter 11.

The end-of-project agendas may focus on gaining approval or a 'GO' status in order to complete the final project activity. These meetings are referred to as 'Go/No GO' calls. The agenda for these meetings focuses on gaining the final resource status in order to move the project forward and generally only take place once all tasks and action items are complete.

There's also a close out meeting which is typically the last meeting for the project team. The close out agenda focuses on any clean up activities required and Lessons Learned from the project. Clean up activities refer to removing old software, making a back up and generally just putting things back where they belong. The Lessons Learned are important for you, as the PM. This is your opportunity to gain feedback from the project stakeholders on your performance as well as the overall project's performance. This is important feedback for you to use on improving future projects. Lessons Learned are covered more thoroughly in Chapter 13.

Deviations from the agenda

Should you allow discussions to deviate from your meeting agenda? It depends...

There are three questions you need to ask yourself when determining if a discussion, which has gone off topic, should continue.
1. Is there enough time allotted to this meeting to allow this conversation to continue? (If you have only a half hour allocated to the meeting, but have a small agenda, you may have time to allow the deviation to continue.)
2. Is the conversation relevant to resolving an issue? (If you can resolve an issue right now, then go for it.)

3. Are all the people required to make a decision related to the issue, on this call? (If everyone necessary is not on the call, then you're likely going to have to repeat this discussion for their sake.)

If the answer to any of the 3 questions is 'no' then you should consider bringing the discussion back to the agenda.

As the leader of the meeting you do not have to constantly rein in the attendees or discussions. Keep control, but hold the reins loosely whenever you can. But if you're on a tight schedule or short on time, by all means pull in the reins and keep strict control.

If you have to bring the discussion back to your agenda, take a note of the topic being discussed and offer to set up a separate meeting to discuss it. It's also possible that the attendees having the off-topic discussion can call each other to work out their issue. If you have faith in them and they wish to do this, allow them, but follow up to make sure it gets done.

Encourage discussion

As the project PM, you need to take a leadership position in the meeting. Your job is to direct the conversation through the agenda, discussing each topic that needs attention. If the conversation consists of only your voice, you may be missing important information. Your meeting participants need to be encouraged to discuss each agenda item and to feel encouraged to speak up.

To effectively encourage participants, treat them as equals. Listen to their input, thank them for participating and ask them open ended questions. An open ended question such as "What is holding us back from completing task #22 now?" encourages participants to respond. Good questions start with why, how and what. Also, it is important to maintain a positive, inviting atmosphere. If someone is not speaking up, ask them their opinion. If there was not a lot of discussion during the call, make sure to end the call by asking each person individually if they have anything to add.

The worst thing you can do is run your meeting as a disciplinarian. This leads others to shut down and keep their mouths closed. When participants do this, it is guaranteed that something important will be missed.

Disagreement is healthy too because it brings opposing views into a forum where they can be vetted. The pros and cons can be explored. If everyone agreed, there would never be anything new, efficiencies would not be gained, and knowledge would be lost. If no consensus is reached, try a temporary trial period for one or the other view. If it succeeds, then you have a new avenue to success. If it fails, then you know for sure that it does not work.

Chapter 8 takeaway
- Set the agenda.
    - Kickoff agenda, 'driving' agenda, End of project agenda.
- Ask yourself three questions when the discussion begins to go off-topic.
    1. Is there enough time allotted to this meeting to allow this conversation to continue?
    2. Is the conversation relevant to resolving an issue?
    3. Are all the people required to make a decision related to the issue, on this call?
- Maintain a positive, inviting atmosphere and encourage discussion.

9. Risk

You, as the PM, are responsible for identifying and reducing known risks, as well as unknown risks. Once risks are identified, it is important to assess which risks require the development of a risk assessment plan.

A risk plan can be as simple as stating, if 'X' happens, call Mr. Y. Or it can be detailed to the level of having multiple steps to back out of a hardware change and to restore the original configuration. Each risk is unique.

Risk assessment involves assessing which risks may affect your project and to what degree. Risk abatement plans detail how you will reduce risks or address them once they occur.

Hopefully, you will never need to use risk abatement plans.

Known and Unknown Risk

The two types of risk are:
- Known Risk: This is a risk you can foresee, or one that you know has occurred before. A known risk is usually easy to plan for.
  - These are likely risks that occurred before, or cover areas where failure is likely.
  - With proper planning at the beginning of the project, these risks should have little, or no, impact on the project.
- Unknown Risk: This type of risk is everything outside the world of known risk. The unknown risk is difficult and sometimes impossible to plan for, but that doesn't remove the PM's responsibility from addressing any that arise.
  - These could be identified through conversations with SMEs, converting them to known risks.

- o Typically these are discovered only after they occur.
- o If not planned for beforehand, your only course of action is a reactionary one.
- o These require fast reactions to resolve the issue and reduce impact on your project.

Risks range from large issues such as government regulatory rulings that affect how pharmaceutical companies bring new products to market, to smaller issues such as a computer software issue preventing a technician from performing his role. A good method of dealing with risks is to hold a risk assessment call, or after a risk becomes a reality, a risk abatement call with SMEs in order to resolve that risk.

Creating a list of possible risks to your project, followed by assigning a ranking of probability and severity helps identify the important risks you must address.

Probability and Severity

Once your risks are identified, put them into an MS Excel spreadsheet. Next to each risk rank the probability that risk could occur. Next to that column, rank the severity to your project if that risk occurred. Use the ranking system of one through three (1-3), with '3' being the highest probability or severity and '1' being the lowest. In the fourth and last column, total the probability ranking and the severity ranking.

You should have something that looks like this:

Risk	Probability	Severity	Total
First Risk	1	2	3
Second Risk	2	3	5
Third Risk	3	1	4
Fourth Risk	2	2	4

Your 'Total' column identifies which risks have the highest overall risk and impact to your project; the higher the total, the higher the risk. The second risk has a total of 5 (out of a max of 6). This risk has a medium probability of occurring, but has a severe impact on your project if it occurs. This is one risk that you definitely need to plan for. On the other hand, the first risk has a low probability of occurring and a medium level of severity. You may be able to overlook this risk.

Risk Abatement

Depending on the scope of the identified risk, your risk abatement plan can range from simple to grand. In either situation, you need to identify the steps to be taken once a risk has occurred. The steps should spell out enough detail for someone other than yourself to follow (you may not be the one resolving the risk).

A meeting with the project SMEs should be the first step. The SMEs can not only identify potential risks, but will know what steps to take to resolve each risk, should they occur. Other sources for risk abatement plans include the project sponsor, stakeholders and peers that have completed similar work. The important thing to remember is not to develop the risk plans by yourself; use the experience of those around you and share your work with others so that they can help improve your plans.

Your risk plan may include steps to be taken after a risk has become a reality. But, often there are steps that can be taken before a risk becomes reality which would further reduce the impact on the project. The 'pre' steps should be identified as well as the 'post' steps.

A simple Risk plan should include the identified risk, pre-risk steps (pre-planning), and the steps to be taken after the risk has become reality (post-planning). See below for an example risk plan.

Risk Description - Pre-Plan - Post-Plan
First Risk   N/A Take these steps…
Second Risk   Notify X   Call help desk
Third Risk   N/A See documentation

Chapter 9 takeaway
- Known Risks: Risks you are aware of.
- Unknown Risks: All risks existing outside of the ones you know.
- Probability of a risk: The likeliness a risk is to occur.
- Severity of a Risk: How much of an impact a risk would have on your project.
- Probability of a Risk: How likely a risk is to occur.
- Rank Risks according to probability and severity.
- Develop pre-occurrence and post-occurrence Plans for each risk.

A risk assessment plan (with probability and severity) can be found on my website. You can also find a sample risk abatement plan on my website. Both can be found under the Chapter 9 section, at http://www.kasteneric.com/Page6.html.

10. Faults in your project

It is inevitable that your project will have a 'fault'. A primary example of a fault is when somebody fails to complete their portion of the project on time. When this happens, a domino effect occurs and all tasks following the delayed one are also delayed. In this case, task #4 is jeopardizing the rest of the project and is referred to as a jeopardy situation. For example, if task #4 of a 12 task project took 3 days longer than it was supposed to, then most likely tasks 5 through 12 will have to be delayed 3 days as well.

The other type of fault occurs after an activity has taken place but failed or, when a part of the project has not gone according to plan. This type of fault is called a defect. It is a defect in some part of a completed task. For example, if cables are run in a building for a computer network and passed testing, but when computers are connected and have no connectivity due to a bad cable, this is a defect.

Issue (Pre-Jeopardy Situation)

You have a task coming due in 2 days and the person responsible for completing the task has admitted they haven't started yet and it will take them more than 2 days of process time. This is an 'issue'. If they don't complete their task on time you will have a 'jeopardy situation'. Before this 'issue' becomes a 'jeopardy situation' you need to take action. You need to communicate the 'issue' to the resources and stakeholders and identify the 'issue' to them. You can use a formal document, or a simple typed email. Either way, the 'issue' must be communicated to the members of the project.

Contained in the Issue Notification that is communicated you must include:
- Description of the issue.
- The due date of the task causing the issue.

- The date at which the issue becomes a jeopardy situation.
- Description of the impact to the project if the issue is not resolved by the task due date.
- Identify the person/team responsible for completing the task.

The 'issue' is brought to the attention of others to identify a potential fault before that fault occurs. It is not a 'finger pointing' exercise, but it is an identification exercise, or an official project warning. It brings attention to the possibility of a delay causing fault. As a PM, you have individuals outside of your management performing tasks in your project for you. By communicating the 'issue', you give other managers the opportunity to reprioritize their work, or shuffle their people around so that the task can be completed on time and before the 'jeopardy situation' arrives.

An 'issue' is a warning that says, "Hey, we might have a problem." In many cases the issue will be resolved before it becomes a 'jeopardy situation.'

Jeopardy Situation

You can have an 'issue' that does not get resolved, leading you to a 'jeopardy situation'. You could also have a supplier call you and say, "All those widgets you ordered are going to take an extra two weeks to make. Shipping will be delayed two weeks." This too is a 'jeopardy situation'. Jeopardy situations can be foreseen at times. They also can come out of nowhere.

A 'jeopardy situation' is when your project's schedule or scope has been drastically altered from its current planned state in a negative way. You may be in near panic mode when a 'jeopardy situation pops up. Just take a deep breath and focus on communication and recovery.

The first step toward recovery is to analyze the impact of the 'jeopardy situation' you are now in. Then you have to communicate. The 'jeopardy situation' communication carries more weight than the 'issue' communication because it identifies a fault that has occurred and a negative force has already impacted your project.

Your Jeopardy Situation communication should contain the below information:
- Your project's name and brief description.
- Date the Jeopardy Communication has been communicated.
- Description of the jeopardy task and the date it was due.
- The person/team responsible for taking action to resolve your jeopardy situation.
- Description of the impact to the project (delays, cost, etc…).
- New Due Date for correcting the jeopardy situation.

The communication of your jeopardy situation should be formal and should be distributed to the person/team responsible for resolving the jeopardy situation, their management (manger and possibly director), and the project stakeholders. The purpose for communicating the above information is to bring focus to resolving the 'jeopardy situation' quickly.

After the 'jeopardy situation' is resolved, you must re-analyze your project's schedule, scope and cost. If necessary, you may have to create a new schedule, negotiate a new scope or negotiate for additional funding. It all depends on the impact of the 'jeopardy situation' on your project.

Once the 'jeopardy situation' is resolved you also need to communicate that the 'jeopardy situation' has been resolved to the same distribution list you used previously. Make sure to include what action was taken to resolve the 'jeopardy situation'. Also, note the Jeopardy and resolution for review in the lessons learned meeting after the project is finished.

Real life example: When a date is missed, automation is used to email the responsible person that they are responsible for the missed date, to provide a new date, or to mark it as completed. The database is also marked with a Jeopardy flag for that missed date. Automation is a great tool for this.

Defects

Similar to a defective product, projects can have defects too. Unlike the 'jeopardy situation', which is caused by the lack of something happening, the defect is caused after something has taken place. A defect is when an activity or task has occurred and has caused a fault (or failure). Defects can cause a 'jeopardy situation' if future tasks of the project are negatively affected.

Possible defect causes:
- Bad data in an engineering document.
- Failure of a planned activity.
- Equipment not performing at 100% after an activity.
- A cable goes bad after installation.
- Product does not meet specifications.

Similar to the jeopardy communication, the defect should also be formally communicated. Make sure to send it to the appropriate people and inform them of the defect and it's impact on the project. Engage the appropriate SMEs and/or teams responsible to resolve the defect.

Resolving a defect can range from email communications, conference calls, meetings, or acquiring new equipment. The type of defect will determine the course of action needed to resolve. You may be able to reschedule an activity or have someone revise their data. Other times, you may need to host a troubleshooting conference call, or meeting, with the responsible person/team and stakeholders. Your goal is to fix the defect and get the project back on course.

You will need to communicate the resolution of the problem. You will need to include the below information:
- Date of the defect.
- Description of the defect.
- Steps taken to resolve the defect.
- Identify the people/teams involved to resolve the defect.
- Describe the impact to the project.

When troubleshooting the defect, you may have to escalate to higher level teams (if your company has teams to escalate to). It is your responsibility to escalate, or have the correct people perform the escalation as needed. You must drive the resolution and keep the momentum moving towards fixing the defect.

Like the jeopardy situation, make sure to review the defect in the lessons learned meeting after the project is finished.

Document

In addition to sending out emails and communicating a 'jeopardy situation', or defect, it's a good idea to document them. A simple Microsoft Excel document that tracks each instance of an 'issue', 'jeopardy situation' and defect along with the associated dates and resolution notes are all you need. If you don't have a separate tracker for each project, and instead have a single issue tracker, then add a column to identify the associated project.

Your tracking document may look like this:

Date	Item	Resolution Date	Resolution Notes
1/1	Issue #1	1/3	Engineer completed work
2/1	Jeopardy	2/5	Delivered equipment
5/1	Defect #1	5/2	Replaced router

Documentation provides two important benefits for you. First, it provides learning material for future, similar projects. This helps you improve over time and gives you information to share with other PMs who may also benefit. Your tracker is also a good source after your project is completed and you hold a 'Lessons Learned' meeting. You can review each item and ways to avoid problems in the future. Second, Documentation provides a record of your efforts to keep the project on track. This comes in handy when a project finishes in a non-favorable timeframe or with un-favorable results and you have to report to upper management about where the break-down occurred.

Chapter 10 takeaway
- Issue: Pre-'jeopardy situation'. Acts as a warning for potentially negative impact to your project.
- Jeopardy Situation: When your schedule or scope has been negatively, and drastically, impacted. Generally from failure to complete a task/activity on time.
- Defect: Occurs after a task or activity has been completed and has caused a negative impact. Can cause a jeopardy situation to future project tasks.
- Communicate the important information to the right people.
- Document! Document! Document!

A sample fault tracker is provided on my website and can be found under the Chapter 10 section, at
http://www.kasteneric.com/Page6.html.

11. Conflicts and Resistance

Similar to the project faults, it is inevitable that you will experience conflict/resistance as a PM. A PM will experience conflict/resistance due to limited experience in the job, general personality conflicts or lack of subject matter experience. There could also be conflict/resistance between members of your project team. No matter what, you need to create an environment that reduces the likeliness of conflicts/resistance and, when they appear, you need to address them. Some conflict is a good thing and helps broaden the team's thinking and increases diversity thinking. However, too much conflict drags down the project team. There are several ways to reduce the likelihood of conflicts. Each has benefits and each may, or may not, work for you.

Honesty and openness are the first steps towards reducing the likeliness of conflicts or resistance. Be honest with your peers and encourage them to be honest with you. It's okay to admit that you don't know all the steps, or all the process details when asked. You don't need to offer that information to the team without being prompted to, but when it comes up, don't hesitate to state your expertise, or lack thereof. Be honest. People can smell dishonesty, especially if a PM says they know as much as an SME, but they really do not.

If you hide a fact, and someone finds out, they will talk to others. This will start rumors and create an environment where your project team members do not trust you. You must be the 'authority' on your project. Any lack of honesty and openness undermines that. Stay on the high road and set a positive example. It is acceptable to release a fact at the right time, such as waiting for a task to complete before releasing something that could have distracted the team from completing that task.

Immediate action is needed when a negative conflict or resistance is encountered. If there is a conflict between team members or between you and a team member, think about how it can be used positively. If it escalates negatively, take immediate action to resolve the conflict. If someone seems resistant to participate you must immediately contact the person directly and if they continue their resistance, approach their manager. Do not let it fester and grow. A great way to address conflict and prevent it from repeating is to talk to the person, or people, immediately and privately. Dig into the root cause of the conflict/resistance. Let them know that you will not tolerate conflicts or resistance that negatively affect your project.

Honesty and openness along with an immediate response are two ways to maintain a positive environment. There are many more. Find what works best for you and keep looking for additional methods.

Acceptance

Success leads to acceptance. One of the best ways to improve your acceptance as a PM and to increase other's willingness to follow you is through success. Successfully completing projects improves your acceptance.

Although this is difficult for new PMs who have no track record, you must keep this in mind as you complete projects. Starting with smaller, easier projects is a great way to begin building your success record and your acceptance.

Beginning small, building experience and growing into larger, more complex projects is the same as starting a new job at an entry level position and slowly working their way up the food chain to an upper management position. As you grow, your experience, skill, knowledge and ability will increase.

There was a Director at a large telecom company that used to say, "Perception is reality". Well, reality is reality, but someone's perception does influence what they perceive as reality. The good thing is that success does improve people's perception of you. But building a solid foundation and increasing experience improves the reality.

Organizational Culture and Organizational Structure

If your organization is new to project management or matrix organizations, you may encounter resistance. You may have to work against the system to get your project completed. If that is the case, document your efforts and present them to upper management upon completion of your project. When presenting this documentation focus on organizational acceptance of the different demands projects place on an organization. Your efforts should be focused on changes that promote successful future projects. Engagement of teams and a sense of ownership help increase acceptance of the project and drive it to success.

Real life example: In a company that did not have any project management guidelines, lead engineers from several teams, and lead technicians were brought into a pre-kick-off meeting and presented with the goal of the project. The goal was to optimize the use of deployed telecom equipment by reorganizing assignments to that equipment. They were asked if there were additional opportunities for improvements in that geographic area. With their input, two additional improvements were incorporated into the project at no cost. The improvements were incorporated through the engineering required to meet the original goal. Without the lead engineers and technicians, the two additional improvements would not have been known. Incorporating these two additional goals increased their ownership and motivation to complete the project and it helps the project achieve more than originally anticipated.

You don't need to change the organizational structure to be successful, but you do want to influence it. Ideally, the culture of your organization should consider the changes associated with projects and the structure should be flexible enough to accept project management as a tool to accomplish company goals. If not, it is the role of the project manager to drive corporate change to support the success of the project.

Presentations to upper management is a great opportunity for you to improve your acceptance as a PM and to gain attention within the company. This attention will be needed when you escalate Jeopardy Situations and need support to resolve them. Don't accept the status quo. Continue attempts to positively influence your organization.

Difficult Personalities

There always seems to be one person who rubs others the wrong way. There always seems to be a difficult personality put in place just for you. It is Murphy's Law.

Stay positive and treat them equally and directly. When you address your concerns with them, do it one-on-one and face-to-face if possible. Set expectations and let them know what is tolerated, or not tolerated. If you need to go to their manager, let them know first. This is part of the honest and open environment you want to maintain.

Real life example: There was an English-as-a-second-language resource named Alfred who provided engineering documents to a technician named Brad. Brad was implementing the changes identified in the engineering document. Brad called to say that he was having a difficult time communicating with Alfred and couldn't understand him. To take the 'speech' out of the equation they were directed to a three way instant message. It worked great. Accent-free text was used to get to the bottom of the issue and resolve it. The two resources communicated better than they could have on a phone call.

Be creative and always keep on eye out for new solutions to try. Sometimes the best solution is the simplest.

Chapter 11 takeaway
- Create a positive environment.
    o Honesty and openness are great ways to prevent conflict/resistance.
    o Take immediate action to address the conflict/resistance.
- Success leads to acceptance.
- Consider your organizational culture and structure. Influence it to improve project success.
- Constantly look for creative solutions to conflict and resistance.

12. Lessons Learned

After your project is completed you should hold a Lessons Learned meeting. This meeting should include all the people who had been involved in the project. Your agenda should cover all the steps of the project as well as all the project faults. You will want to find and document aspects of your project, as well as your project management style, that could be improved. Don't be shy. This meeting is for you and your future projects.

High Level Review

Stat your meeting with a high level project review. State the project's purpose and scope then determine how well your project met the project's expectations. Get feedback. Others may have a different perspective on how well you met the project expectations.

Task Review

Next, review the tasks identified at the beginning of the project and compare that to the final task list. Did you add additional tasks? Did you identify tasks that were not needed? How well did actual task durations match your schedule? Your project stakeholders will be able to provide feedback to you.

At the end of your project you should use your actual dates/schedule to review the initial schedule you created for the project. This information can be applied to future, similar projects to make their schedules more accurate.

Fault Review

Go through any 'issues', 'jeopardy situations' and defects that you encountered during your project. These are usually the more critical items to cover during your Lessons Learned meeting. Make sure you identify solutions in order to avoid repeating these same faults on future projects. Make sure your stakeholders agree on the proper solutions.

Upon reviewing faults, your stakeholders may provide additional information or new solutions that were not considered when they were working on the project. They may have had time to consider the faults more thoroughly, or may have had further discussions on the faults that led to better solutions. Either way, allow each fault to be discussed and take notes.

Conflicts

You may want to document any conflicts you encountered during your project, for your personal information. These may or may not be appropriate for group discussion. If they are appropriate for group discussion, put the conflict on the agenda and review it (such as a conflict with a supplier). Keep your eye on solutions and don't allow finger pointing. Address the issue, not the people.

Project Improvement

Throughout your Lessons Learned meeting, keep the group focused on ways to improve the project and your project management style. Encourage them to provide positive feedback to you or to each other. If you could have done something differently in your management of the project, that's good stuff to know and apply to future projects.

Areas for consideration could include methods of communication, tools used throughout the project, additional tasks or checklist items that could reduce risk, etc… Encourage an open discussion and don't let anything said, discourage you from putting yourself out there. If something said comes across as harsh or critical to you, take it with a grain of salt. They wouldn't be telling you if they didn't have faith in your ability to improve. All this information is for your benefit and if used wisely, will make you a better PM. When they see that you implement changes due to their feedback and future projects perform better, they will have faith in your project management ability.

Document and Incorporate

During your lessons learned meeting, write everything down. Ask a co-worker to write things down for you if you think you'll be busy listening or running the meeting.

When the meeting is over, immediately (while everything is still fresh in your mind) update your project plans. Add notes where areas for improvement were identified. Create an updated schedule or add notes to your existing schedule.

Document so that you can easily reference this material next time you perform a similar project. Keep in mind that you will be referencing this material at a later time and don't abbreviate or assume you'll remember everything later. Assume you'll forget, or better yet, assume someone else will be using these notes.

These notes will become part of your project management archive and will serve as a resource on future projects.

Chapter 12 takeaway
- Document all lessons learned from your project. This will help improve your skills as a PM.
- Lessons Learned Agenda:
    - High level review.
    - Tasks review.
    - Fault review.

- - Conflicts (if appropriate).
  - Overall Project improvement.
- Document! Document! Document!

13. Putting it all Together

Now that you have all the parts, how do you put them together? There are many steps, some of which can overlap, or take place concurrently. Sometimes some steps have to be repeated. On your first project it's best to take things slowly, one step at a time. After completing a few projects you will know your strengths, find the path that works best for you and will have established some best practices.

Project Start

At the start of your project you need to establish the 'why' of your project. Why is the project needed? This will usually come from the project sponsor or the project initiator. But you need to know why you're doing this work. Why is it a benefit to the company? This is critical when your schedule conflicts with another project's schedule and you need to coordinate which project takes priority over the other. It also helps when you have to explain the importance of completing tasks when they are due. If the project is initiated by you, knowing the 'why' helps you sell the project to upper management.

You will also need to establish the project's scope. The scope sets the target for project completion. Put another way, the scope identifies when your project is done. When all the parts of the scope are met, your project is complete. If the scope is to install an ATM at bank number 231 and make it operational for customers, then you clearly understand when your project is completed. Once you have your scope, confirm any questions you have with the project sponsor and document his responses. Documenting the scope is important later in the project if additional requirements are added and your scope increases (you'll need to renegotiate more time to complete, and/or additional funding).

You may be presented with a simple installation of a new device in a single location, or a complicated world-wide distribution of new equipment. Either way, you will need to know why you're doing what it is you're doing, who the project's sponsor is, and what the full scope of the project is.

Plan it out

This is where you will start putting your project management skills to use. A variety of organizational skills are needed to make the project run smoothly and to help simplify your project. If you don't have experience with organization, this is the perfect opportunity to set a solid foundation and to begin establishing solid organizational practices for yourself.

The first item to tackle is identifying the tasks. The tasks should be mapped out in the order they need to be completed. Identify which can be completed in parallel or which need to be completed in series. This task map will be the foundation for the rest of your planning. Use SMEs to confirm and refine your tasks. Keep in mind that if this is the first time a certain type of project is being performed, you may have to add, or modify, tasks later.

Once the tasks are identified you need to put them on a schedule and identify resources. Part of the schedule may have to be finalized later and some of the resources may not be able to be identified until later. If either of these has to be completed at a later time, identify the missing data on your documentation and make notes for yourself to follow up on them. A good way to do this is to add the missing data as an agenda item to your meetings, leaving it on the agenda until the missing data is acquired.

Next, you will need to complete some planning specific to your style of project management and include consideration of

the organizational structure and its culture. Ask yourself the below questions.
1. How will changes need to be tracked and how will I react to them?
2. How will project communication be handled?
3. How will project faults be handled and tracked?
4. How will risks to the project be addressed?
5. Is there a potential for conflict within the project team? If so, are there steps that can be taken now to reduce the conflict later?

Answer these questions, and document how you will address each one. Use this documentation to establish processes for all your projects. Use what works best for you (within the parameters of your organization) and you will increase your success rate as well as simplify your work. You can take these questions a step further and communicate them to your project stakeholders so they too know what to expect from you as a project manager. When the time comes and you need to address change, or one of the other topics, you will already know what you need to do.

Another part of planning out your project is to identify any corporate tools that you have to use and/or update. There may be financial, task, or project tools that you are required to keep updated so that your company can track your project along with other projects. You may need to send an MS Excel document to somebody, or update an online application. Identifying these tools now will keep negative attention from impacting you later. Document these tools and identify when they require input. Updating a tool can even be a task in your project that is assigned to you.

When you feel confident that all the planning that can be done is done, revisit your scope. Make sure your scope is fully addressed by your plan. Also, identify tasks that fall outside your scope. Any differences between your scope and your tasks should be addressed with the project sponsor and the stakeholders before you begin executing on your plans.

Time to Execute

You have a solid plan for your project. Now it's time to execute. This step is going to be specific to whatever tasks you planned for your project. The most important part of this step is to take the lead and steer the project towards completion. This means gaining consensus between departments, motivating the team and being the champion that does whatever it takes to successfully complete the project.

You may be required to work days and nights, maybe even weekends. As long as you're leading and making sure team members are doing what they need to do to complete your project, you're doing the right thing. Sometimes you may be required to be hands-on in order to get the job done, but mainly you should be the person driving, not the mechanic changing the tire.

Take the initiative and do your best to not be reactionary (even though reactionary is sometimes unavoidable). If you find yourself acting like a fireman (constantly putting out fires) you should take a step back and review your project plan, looking for opportunities to prevent those fires. Continuously look ahead within your project. Identify upcoming tasks and make sure there are no roadblocks to prevent them from starting on time. Look further down the road and make sure your project is heading in the right direction. Take the time to make predictions and identify potential risks. Keep an eye on those risks and address them head-on to reduce their impact.

If necessary, you will have to revisit, and possibly revise, your project scope.

Administrative

The administrative portion of your project will take place mostly during the execution phase. There are many administrative tasks to perform during your project. This is where you will be hosting meetings, communicating, and making sure your project is headed in the right direction. Some of the tasks you will need to perform administratively were mentioned in the 'Time to Execute' section.

The first two items to address are the most important and apply to all the rest; Communication and Documentation. Communication is critical to the success of your project. Finding the best wording, length, detail level, etc... is important and takes time. Make sure you get feedback on the effectiveness of your communication so you can optimize it for your organization. Documentation is not only critical to your current project, it's also critical to long term project management improvement. Learning from past projects is the best way to ensure success of future projects.

You will be hosting meetings on your project, either in-person, or over the phone (or web). This is the opportunity to coordinate tasks (such as resource or schedule) between multiple people or departments. Meetings should be open for two-way communication; from you and to you. Your meetings should start with a kick-off meeting, end with a lessons learned meeting and in between these two, you should be hosting sufficient meetings to keep everyone informed and to keep your project on schedule. You will find many agenda items to easily fill your meetings. If you have no agenda items and your project is moving along like a speeding train on a clear track, don't host a call and waste everyone's time.

In the background, you will be performing tasks, such as risk assessment, measuring progress, addressing conflicts, reviewing and refining upcoming tasks, monitoring for scope creep and updating your schedule. These are daily responsibilities of the PM. Each of these tasks will play a part in keeping your project on schedule and increasing the odds that you will be successful.

If necessary, you will have to revisit, and possibly revise, your project scope, as well as your project plan.

Project Completion

Once your project is completed, make sure you have met expectations. Do this by comparing the project scope to the final product. Confirm that all tasks were completed, checklists were completed, and that any clean-up work has been completed. If you find any discrepancies between your completed project and the project scope, address them.

After confirming that the project scope has been met, you will need to host one more meeting; the 'Lessons Learned' meeting. In this meeting the project stakeholders, resources and anyone else involved should be providing you with feedback on what worked, what didn't work, and what sort-of worked. Document everything and implement the feedback that you find most useful, making sure it fits within your organization. Make sure to cover tasks, PM performance, meetings, schedule, etc… in your 'Lessons Learned' meeting.

Lastly, Archive your documentation for future reference. There are many ways to do this; such as updating 'living documents', saving to a hard drive or shared drive, or sending to a central person/department within your organization. Just make sure that you can easily access the documents next time you need them.

Final Remarks

Start with the basics and take it one step at a time. As you progress through your project management career you will find what works best for you. When you find something that doesn't work, look for an alternative. It will be your initiative and your leadership that drives a project to a successful completion. And, always make sure to identify and sincerely thank your project team for everything they do. Without a solid team behind you, you will find it extremely difficult to succeed.

For supporting documentation, please visit my Basics of Project Management website at www.KastenEric.com.

Chapter 13 takeaway
- Step 1 : Project Start
    - Establish the 'why'.
    - Establish who the project sponsor is.
    - Establish and document the project scope.
- Step 2 : Plan it out
    - Map out the project tasks.
    - Create initial schedule.
    - Identify resources.
    - How will changes be tracked?
    - What are the communication plans?
    - How will project faults be addressed?
    - How will risks be addressed?
    - Is there a potential for conflict on your project team?
    - What corporate tools will you be required to use?
    - If necessary, revisit the project scope.
- Step 3 : Time to Execute
    - Take the lead. Steer project towards completion.

- - o Take the initiative… look ahead, predict, and avoid risk…
  - o Be the champion!
- Step 4 : Administrative (Takes place during project execution)
  - o Communicate!
  - o Document!
  - o Meetings.
  - o Risk assessment.
  - o Measure progress.
  - o Address conflicts.
  - o Refine tasks as they get closer.
  - o Keep schedule updated and revise if needed.
  - o Watch out for scope creep.
  - o If necessary, revisit project scope.
  - o If necessary, revisit project plan.
- Step 5 : Project Completion
  - o Confirm project met expectations, scope is satisfied.
  - o Lessons learned meeting.
  - o Archive project for future reference.

For your reference, these 5 steps are also listed on my website and can be found under the Chapter 13 section, at http://www.kasteneric.com/Page6.html.

14. Project Metrics

Now that you have the means to manage a project, how do you measure performance of a project, or multiple projects? Organizations may have metrics pre-defined for PMs to achieve. Sometimes a PM may have several similar projects to manage and needs a way to assess how the projects compare to each other. Either way, a metric should always be quantitative.

Cycle Time Metrics

A cycle time metric measures a timeframe between two end points, such as how many days between a start and an end date. The days could be measure in calendar days or business days. Another example could be hold time for a customer service company, such as measuring minutes between call initiation and call pick up by a representative, or to the end of the call.

The cycle times of all instances are averaged to get the average cycle time of whatever start and end points measured. A target cycle time average is then compared to that calculated average cycle time. This type of metric is good for encouraging PMs to reduce the measured timeframe. It allows cycle times greater than the target and places importance on the overall average.

Example:
If you are managing the construction of cellular sites, you may use this...
Start Date = Construction start
End Date = Construction End
(Measured in calendar days)
Cycle Time = Construction End Date - Construction Start Date
Target cycle time = 85 days

If construction started April 1 and ended July 1, the cycle time would be 91 days.

If there are 100 sites, the cycle time of all 100 sites would be averaged and compared to the target of 85 days.

An average cycle time can be below target and still have less instances of meeting the target if those cycle times are very small, such as 70% of sites could be greater than the target if the 30% that make target are very small cycle times. If this is acceptable, then this metric works.

Met/Miss Metrics

Met/Miss metrics are either yes or no, or "1" or "0". This metric is specific to how many times a metric target is achieved such as, how many times a customer service representative answered a call within 30 seconds or less versus how many times the representative answered a call greater than 30 seconds. If the call was answered 30 seconds or less, the metric would record a "1" and if the call was answered after 30 seconds, the metric would record a "0".

Using the same example as above:
If you are managing the construction of cellular sites, you may use this…
Start Date = Construction start
Measurement = 85 days from construction start
If construction end is less than or equal to 85 then record a "1"
If construction end more than 85 then record a "0"
(Measured in calendar days)
Target = Achieve measurement more than 90% of the time

If construction started April 1 and ended July 1, the result would be 91 days and the metric would be a 0.

If construction started April 1 and ended June 1, the result would be 61 days and the metric would be a 1.

If there are 100 sites and 93 finished less than or equal to 85 days, the results would be calculated as a percentage of the total, 93 / 100 = .93 or 93%. The results are 93% of the time construction finished less than or equal to 85 days. In this case, the target of 90% success is achieved, since 93% is greater than 90%.

This metric does not consider how far beyond the 85 days construction took when this metric was missed. Average cycle time could have been more than 100 days. The sites that missed the construction measurement of 85 days could have taken 200+ days, but they have the same impact as sites finishing at 86 days… both get a "0".

Making a cycle time metric does not mean you will make a met/miss metric on the same criteria, and vice-versa.

Applying Metrics to Projects

There are several ways to apply metrics to projects. The obvious metric would be to measure the overall project, but is it more important to measure the cycle time of the projects, or to measure the percent of times projects complete on time… or both?

Measuring the cycle time may be more important if capturing the overall length of time it takes to complete projects. Measuring success may be more important if capturing individual performance of project managers.

Measuring the overall project with a metric is good, but remains at a high level. It does not provide a granular view of what is happening within a project. It is beneficial to place metrics between milestones. These milestone metrics help identify where within a project issues exist.

For example, 100 construction projects can have their on time completion metric analyzed and the result could be 89% on a target of 90%. This indicates 11 sites did not complete on time. It does not say why those 11 sites missed the metric.

If the milestones metrics of those 11 sites were analyzed, it could look like this:

Const start to foundation complete = 98%
Foundation complete to framing/siding complete = 96%
Framing/siding complete to roofing complete = 50%
Roofing complete to plumbing & electrical complete = 99%
Plumbing & electrical complete to interior complete = 89%

In this example, something caused the roofing to complete on time only 50% of the time. Was it weather related? Was the expected time to complete underestimated? These milestone level metrics give much more information than just an overall on time percentage.

Metric Weighting

Weighting of metrics help identify which metrics are more important by carrying more weight. Without weighting, every metric would be considered equal. The below example takes the construction example and applies weighting to it. More weight is given to completing the framing/siding and completing the roofing. These 2 steps are more important to complete on time so that the subsequent activities can be completed within the enclosed structure.

Const start to foundation weight = 15%
Foundation complete to framing/siding weight = 30%
Framing/siding complete to roofing weight = 30%

Roofing complete to plumbing & electrical weight = 15%
Plumbing & electrical complete to interior weight = 10%
- The total weight should add up to 100% -

Multiplying the weight of the metric times the metric result gives a weighted result. Adding all the weighted results together gives a percentage of success. In the above example, Framing/siding complete to roofing complete on time percentage = 50% and the weight is 30%. Multiplying 30% weight times 50% success results in a 15% weighted result.

The following chart illustrates these on time percentages and weights and shows that the 100 projects completed with an overall weighted result of 82%.

Metric	Weighting	Metric Results	Weighted Results
Construction start to foundation complete on time percentage	15%	98%	**15%**
Foundation complete to framing/siding complete on time percentage	30%	96%	**29%**
Framing/siding complete to roofing complete on time percentage	30%	50%	**15%**
Roofing complete to plumbing & electrical complete on time percentage	15%	99%	**15%**
Plumbing & electrical complete to interior complete on time percentage	10%	89%	**9%**
			82%

Chapter 14 takeaway
- Cycle Time metric
    o Measures an average of completion timeframes.
    o Good for measuring an overall view of multiple projects.
- Met/Miss metric
    o Measures the percent on time against the total.
    o Good for measuring individual performance.
- Applying to projects
    o Do you need a project start to finish metric?
    o Do you need milestone level metrics?
    o Do you need both?
- Weighting
    o Gives more importance to certain metrics instead of leaving them to be of equal importance.

Thank you for reading my book. I hope you found useful information within these pages! Please take a moment to provide a positive review on amazon.com and to check out my website at www.kasteneric.com.

References:
"What is Project Management?", Project Management Institute. Retrieved May 24, 2012 from www.pmi.org

www.ingramcontent.com/pod-product-compliance
Lightning Source LLC
Chambersburg PA
CBHW070120210526
45170CB00013B/826